This Guidebook belongs to: _____

Contents

LESSON 1

■ Pick a kitchen tool, and think about how it relates to being a dad.

1. What does it make you think of?
2. Describe how it represents your role as a dad.

Wooden Spoon	Measuring Cup

Apron	Cast Iron Skillet

Whisk	Blender

Measuring Spoons	Oven Mit

Reflection Questions

1. What did you learn about food and cooking growing up? Who did you learn from?

2. What did you learn from other men about health and taking care of your body?

3. How do you think your health habits affect your children's health and habits?

LESSON 2

Create safety by regulating yourself, helping children to regulate, and establishing a safe environment.

There are 3 types of regulation:

1. **Other-regulation:** Children are dependent on an adult for regulation, i.e., swaddling and rocking a baby, singing a song, holding or touching.

2. **Co-regulation:** Children are wired to imitate and emulate your actions, so if you are regulated, that will help them regulate themselves. Dysregulated people cannot help others regulate.

3. **Self-regulation:** This is a taught skill, so children will need to have some guidance and practice as to what and how to self-regulate. They need to experience #1 and #2 in order to learn self-regulation.

Help yourself and others regulate by creating a safe environment that is:

» Calm

» Connected

» Nonjudgmental

» Predictable

» Supportive

Remember

Children may feel internally unsafe even in safe environments. Trust and connection are built with your consistency over time.

The human body is built to handle stress...some of the time. Common symptoms of short-term stress include:

The **brain** may get distracted with repetitive thoughts, making it difficult to concentrate

The **head** may start to hurt; some people become extra sensitive to light and sound

Vision may get blurry, eyelids may twitch, or eyes may hurt

Teeth may clench and the mouth may dry out

Muscles may tense or tremble

Heart rate increases along with blood pressure; this makes it difficult to sleep

Skin may get pale, sweaty, or flushed

Breathing may speed up and become shallow; some people hold their breath

Appetite may go up or down; some people experience nausea or even stomach pain

Bowel and bladder control are reduced during extreme stress

Positive Stress	*Tolerable Stress*	*Toxic Stress*
This stress response isn't always damaging. Positive stress occurs with a change or situation you want, such as starting a new job or traveling to a new place. In these situations, a little stress can be motivating.	Tolerable stress occurs when our bodies respond to more serious threats, such as injury or arguments, but return to a regulated state easily. Coping skills, loving support, and good health help the body return to a regulated state.	When stress is very severe or lasting, however, the body cannot easily return to a calm state. This is toxic stress. Over time, toxic stress can lead to poor physical and emotional health.

> **Did you know?** A well-balanced diet is like building a fire with logs instead of sticks—your fire will burn brighter and stronger.

What can put out your fire too fast?

Our bodies crave sugar, salt, caffeine, or highly processed snacks when stressed, tired, or "down" because they provide quick energy and/or pleasure. But these foods can also cause a crash when the feeling wears off, ultimately making our energy or mood worse. We may also skip meals when anxious, tired, or in a hurry. This can cause mood or energy crashes, often leading to overeating unhealthy food later.

Improve your mood and energy with good food.

» A diet rich in whole foods provides the necessary vitamins, minerals, fiber, and other nutrients needed to support a healthy gut microbiome, the vagus nerve, and nervous system function.

» Protein fills you up and provides amino acids needed for steady moods.

» Vitamins and minerals from colorful fruits and vegetables can help the body stay strong and adapt to stress.

» Eating balanced snacks or meals regularly during your day can keep your energy and mood from plummeting.

» Drinking water improves mood and concentration. It also helps bring nutrients to your muscles so your body can feel more energized.

Flavored Water Recipe

» Fill a pitcher with cool water
» Add ½ cup thinly sliced cucumber and ½ cup fresh mint leaves
» Chill in the refrigerator
» Enjoy!

Try different combinations of flavors:

1. Thin slices: lemon, lime, orange, grapefruit, cucumber, apple, berries, melon, pineapple, fresh ginger
2. Fresh leaves/sprigs: mint, basil, rosemary, parsley

This cheat sheet presents some basics of healthy eating. Check it out. Do you see any of your favorite foods??

WHOLE GRAINS & OTHER COMPLEX CARBOHYDRATES

Some carbohydrates are "complex." That means they take a lot of work for your body to break down. They also provide your body with more nutrients and help you feel full longer.

Examples: brown rice, whole wheat products (bread, tortillas), oatmeal, quinoa, amaranth, lentils, beans, starchy fruits and vegetables

HEALTHY FATS

The human body needs different kinds of fats for health. Without fat, the body cannot use some vitamins. Children's brains need healthy fats too. Fats are also slow to digest. This can help you stay full for a long time. Choose fats that have been minimally or not at all processed.

Examples: avocados, whole nuts and nut butters (low-salt or unsalted), peanuts and peanut butter, olives and olive oil, seeds, fatty fish like salmon and sardines

COLORFUL VEGETABLES

Different colored vegetables and fruits have different nutrients. To get a variety, try to "eat the rainbow" every day. Enjoy them raw and cooked in different ways, too. Enjoy leafy greens as often as possible.

[continues on next page...]

WHOLE FRUITS

Whole, fresh fruits contain natural sugars in small amounts. These sugars give quick energy and have vitamins, minerals, and fiber. Choose colorful fruits. Enjoy them raw or minimally cooked.

PROTEIN FROM PLANTS

Whether you're a vegetarian or not, enjoy some protein from plants. These foods often have more fiber and less saturated fat than foods that come from animals. They can also be cheaper and last longer.

Examples: beans, lentils, nuts and nut butters, seeds and seed butters, tofu and tempeh

HEALTHY BEVERAGES

Water is the perfect drink for a healthy body. If you want something else for a change, drink beverages made with clean water, unsweetened milk or milk substitutes, and whole, natural foods. They can be flavored with fruits, herbs, spices or vanilla extract.

Examples: water flavored with fresh fruit, iced or hot herbal teas, unsweetened milk and milk substitutes (i.e. almond, soy)

THINK ABOUT IT

» What are your go-to "Do Eat" foods?

» What foods can you swap out and replace with these healthy choices?

» What is a simple meal you could make with 2 or more ingredients from these categories?

■ **A snack is like a small meal and should be just as nutritious as your meals.**

» Plan ahead and carry a healthy snack with you when you are going out for a long time.

» Keep quick and easy snacks around such as frozen fruit, bananas, nuts, cheese sticks or slices, hummus, or whole grain crackers.

» Make sure you drink enough water! Dehydration can also contribute to low energy.

■ **Mood & Energy Boosting Snacks**

» Try pairing a protein or healthy fat with a carbohydrate to boost mood and energy and satisfy hunger.

Protein and Healthy Fats:

» raw or toasted nuts
» sunflower or pumpkin seeds
» peanut butter or almond butter
» avocado
» cheese (slices, string cheese, etc.)
» cottage cheese
» hummus or bean dip
» greek yogurt
» hard boiled eggs
» edamame (soybeans)
» glass of milk

+

Carbohydrates:

Fruits and Vegetables:
» sliced apples, grapes, bell pepper, cucumber, cherry tomatoes, carrot sticks, and celery sticks

Whole Grains:
» whole grain crackers, baked tortilla chips, whole wheat tortillas, popcorn, whole grain granola bars

Quick & Easy Snack Ideas

Quick Quesadilla: Spread refried beans on a tortilla, add grated cheese. Microwave, add salsa, hot sauce, or avocado.

Snack Mix: Mix together unsweetened ready-to-eat cereal, dried fruit, and nuts in a sandwich bag for an on-the-go snack.

Hummus (Bean Dip) & Veggies: Scoop up hummus (or another bean dip) with your favorite cut veggies (e.g., carrot and celery sticks, cucumber slices, jicama)

Yogurt Fruit Parfait: Top low-fat yogurt with cut-up fruit and a little granola or dried cereal.

Baked Potato: Microwave small baking potato. Top with grated cheese and salsa.

Tuna Salad & Veggies: Mix canned tuna with a little mayonnaise, lemon juice, diced celery, and onion. Enjoy with cucumber slices or crackers. Try this with canned chicken!

The easiest snack could also be your leftovers from another meal!

What goes into a balanced diet?

You might be familiar with this model from the USDA. What foods fall in each category?

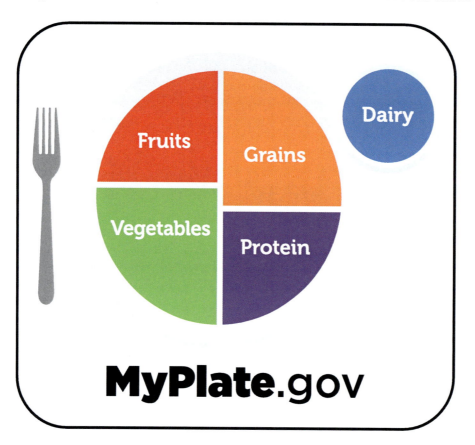

MyPlate recommendations.

» Fill half your plate with fruits and vegetables.

» Eat different kinds of vegetables—dark green as well as other colors.

» Eat whole fruits.

» Make half of your grains whole grains.

» Vary your protein sources to include beans and peas, tofu, nuts, seafood, eggs, and lean meats.

» Choose foods and beverages with less added sugars, saturated fats, and sodium.

» Consume low-fat or fat-free dairy milk or yogurt (or fortified, non-dairy versions).

Source: www.dietaryguidelines.gov

How do you find trustworthy nutritional information online?

Trustworthy sites typically do not have advertisements and come from a reputable medical, educational, or professional organization–the web address usually ends in .edu, .gov, or .org.

EatFresh.org is funded by CalFresh (USDA) and makes shopping and home cooking easy.

Go to *www.EatFresh.org* to start exploring!

» Find healthy, inexpensive, and quick recipes.

» Print, save, share, and text recipes to your mobile phone.

» Learn lifestyle tips to keep you healthy and feeling your best.

» Submit a question to the EatFresh.org dietitian.

» Save time planning and shopping with meal plans.

» Apply for SNAP/CalFresh.

» Learn basic cooking skills and how to substitute ingredients to use what you already have at home.

» View the website in multiple languages.

» View nutritional information for each recipe.

LESSON 3

Which of these statements do you hear more often? What are some ideas about fathers feeding their kids that you think are not true?

1. "Men and women are equally capable of feeding kids."

2. "It's better for fathers to stay out of the way when it comes to cooking for or feeding children."

How we feed can support good mental health and eating habits for everyone in the family.

Feeding styles that create stressful interactions and promote poor eating habits:

» Are highly controlling, too permissive, or neglectful

» Regularly use food as a reward or to soothe

» Use food to punish

The most balanced approaches to feeding feature:

» Adults' behaviors and an environment that model desirable habits and warm interactions

» Consistency and predictability around meals

» Adults taking primary responsibility for offering a balance of foods

» Adults who gently guide a child to make their own reasonable choices

Which of these feeding styles is most likely to promote balanced eating in children?

Which ones create added stress for caregiver or child?

The "Clean Your Plate" Style

» Telling a child how much and what foods they should eat

» Having little trust in child's innate ability to know when they are full/hungry

» Bribing, counting bites, not letting the child leave the table until the adult decides

» Punishing the child for not eating

The "Fly By The Seat of Their Pants" Style

» Has very little structured support around food

» Meals are often unplanned, untimely, and unreliable

The "Yes"/"Short-Order Cook" Style

» Catering to the child's wants at mealtime

» Offering little structure to snacking, leading to child grazing throughout the day

The "Division of Responsibility" Style

» Having reasonable expectations and structure to feeding

» Responsive to a child's needs but allowing the child to make food choices based on their fullness and preferences

» Supporting children's developing autonomy around what goes in their bodies

---

Being clear on the roles and responsibilities of the food provider (you) and the eater (the child) can be helpful in reducing stressful interactions around mealtimes.

Of course, as a caregiver, you can enlist others in your home to support your role!

You are responsible for - *what, when, and where*	Children are responsible for - *how much and whether*
» Choosing and preparing the food » Providing regular and consistent meals » Modeling desired behaviors » Being considerate of children's preferences and lack of food experience » Making mealtimes pleasant » Preventing mindless grazing between meals and snacks (except for purposeful grazing allowed by the parent for medical or sensory reasons) » Letting children grow into the right body for them. Remember, bodies vary!	» What they will eat » Learning when their body tells them they are full » Learning from your role modeling » Growing predictably » Learning to try their best at mealtime

This model was developed by Ellyn Satter, MA, RD, LCSW, BCD.

Self-Reflection:

» Which feeding habits do you identify with?

» Do you have a mixture of feeding styles?

» How is your approach different or the same as how you were fed as a child?

» Has your feeding style ever conflicted with a child in your home?

» Has your feeding style caused stress for you?

» Are there life circumstances that have influenced or changed your feeding style?

» How have you adapted your feeding style?

Young children learn by imitation. Enjoy eating fruits, veggies, and whole grains; and eventually your kids will, too!

Toddlers...

» are growing teeth but are still at high risk for choking.

» may change tastes and appetite from day to day.

» may prefer foods in their simplest form (without sauce or mixed with other foods).

» like to "play" with food using all their senses; plan for this rather than discouraging it.

» can practice self-feeding, drinking from a regular cup, and using utensils. It might be messy at first, but they will learn to feed themselves—saving you some effort later on.

Preschoolers...

» may need to be exposed to new foods many times before acceptance.

» are ready for more structured mealtimes and food routines.

» are more exposed to processed foods outside the home but can begin to learn about healthy decision-making.

What to Offer

» 16-24 oz whole milk per day for kids 12-24 months. Switch to low-fat at 24 months.

» If a child has a cow's milk allergy, choose unsweetened and fortified milk alternatives or toddler formula.

» After age 1, tummies can handle berries, tomatoes, citrus, and honey.

» Three meals plus two healthy snacks per day at predictable times.

» Mild versions of whatever the rest of the family is eating. It's not necessary to cook a separate menu.

» Offer cut-up fruit instead of juice. Fruit juice is not necessary and can harm children's teeth. Juice should not be introduced to infants before 1 year. Limit daily intake to 4 ounces for toddlers ages 1-3 years and 4-6 ounces for ages 4-6 years. If you do serve juice, try diluting no more than 1/4 cup (4 oz) of 100% fruit juice with water and serve in a cup, not a bottle.

Older kids want to do things and eat as their peers do but still need you to provide guidance and nourish their brains and bodies.

Elementary School Kids...

» are beginning to understand where food comes from and that some foods are good for growing bodies.

» need to be active every day for physical and mental health.

» may feel guilty about eating animals.

» benefit from structured mealtimes as they develop decision-making skills.

Adolescents...

» need to be active every day for physical and mental health.

» may start to see connections between diet, physical appearance, and health.

» may be more adventurous with food choices.

» are vulnerable to peer pressure around what to eat and how to look.

» may gain weight more rapidly with the onset of adult hormones.

Make Fruits and Vegetable Fun

» Keep a bowl of fresh fruit on the kitchen table.

» Put washed and cut fruits and veggies on a shelf in your refrigerator where your child can see them.

» Let them pick fruits and veggies at the store.

» Experiment with dips and powdered spices to make these foods more interactive.

Here are some important things to consider when it comes to your child's body size and weight.

Children's weight may fluctuate due to:

» **Growth spurts** - children's bodies will naturally need more food before a growth spurt to get the nutrients and energy needed to fuel the growth process.

» **Puberty** - along with growth spurts, boys and girls have hormonal changes that may change their bodies and weight.

» **Medications** - some medications for mental health and other conditions can alter body composition, metabolism, and hunger cues. If you are concerned about your child's medication, speak with your prescribing doctor.

Beware of weight-loss approaches that encourage an extremely restrictive diet and lifestyles that are difficult to maintain long-term. Over time, they may slow down metabolism and hurt your child's relationship with food and their body.

Seek advice from a registered dietitian who can work with you and your child more closely to build a healthy relationship with food and support health goals.

Caring for Our Bodies

There are important and joyful ways to care for our bodies that can improve our confidence, strength, and energy, as well as contribute to a comfortable weight for you.

» Moving as much as possible—even for short bursts during the day

» Paying attention to how certain foods impact mood and energy levels

» Getting a good night's sleep

» Exposing our bodies to nature and sunshine

» Noticing when media images and advertisements promote negative thoughts about one's own body—feel free to block them!

» Giving appreciation for what our bodies can do

» Giving and getting physical touch and affection, like hugs

Here are some responses to guide your conversations about your child's body size and weight.

Concern	Responses
Your child says: *"I am fat"* - OR - *"I need/want to lose weight"* - OR - *"I hate my body"*	» "How do you feel about the word fat or skinny? » "Why do you think having a different body would be better?" » "Thank you for sharing your feelings with me. It's normal to sometimes feel dissatisfied with our body, want to make changes, or compare ourselves with others." » "How do you see yourself? Do **you** like who you see?"
A family member brings up concerns about your child's weight	» "I appreciate your concern, but their pediatrician is happy with their health status at this time. We aren't concerned with body size issues, just their health." » "I would appreciate it if we did not discuss the topic of weight or size in front of my child. In our home, we focus on health rather than body size."
The pediatrician brings up concerns about your child's weight	» "I understand you are concerned. Are there lab markers or current health issues I need to be aware of that are driving your concerns?" » "I would be happy to discuss any medical concerns through email or a private phone call. Then, we can discuss how to appropriately address them."
Another child calls your child fat	» "What do you think about the comment?" » "I can hear that comment was hurtful to you. I am so sorry that happened." » "I hear you are worried about how other kids see you, but how do **you** see yourself?"
You are concerned about your child's weight	» Evaluate why you are concerned. Are there external influences that inform your concern? » Avoid any mention of weight or body size. If you are wondering whether there might be a health issue, talk to the pediatrician, not the child. » If needed, ask your health provider for resources. If available, talk to a weight-neutral nutritionist. » Focus on healthy living, getting energized and active, and eating nourishing food rather than body size. » Include the entire family in healthy changes. But don't shame each other's food choices.
Your child makes a negative comment about someone else's appearance	**Consider:** » Do you make comments about other people's body or appearance? » Do you make comments about your own body or appearance? » Are there other people in your child's life that comment on the bodies or appearance of other people, or your child?

■ Why do you like to move?

For good health, kids need 60 minutes of exercise daily. Adults need 150 minutes of moderate activity per week or 75 minutes of vigorous activity per week.

» Limit screen time (mobile devices, computer, TV, video games). The hours of screen time per week is directly connected to poor health.

» Physical activity builds strength and endurance. It also improves mood, sleep, energy, and concentration!

» If you have a tough time getting motivated, look for ways to be active with others— find a class, go for walks, dance with a buddy, or add physical games to a family party. Anything that involves movement is better than sitting and watching a screen.

■ Movement for everyday life

» Jump rope

» Jumping jacks

» Dance parties

» Housework

» Stairs instead of the elevator

» Stretching while you brush your teeth

» Take a walk while you are on the phone

"Nothing happens until something moves."
 - Albert Einstein

■ Want to increase your movement?

Make an easy to accomplish goal.

This month I will _____ , _____ times, every _____ .

LESSON 4

How does the layout of your grocery store shape your choices?
Where are the healthiest foods located?
Are products displayed at the ends of aisles always on sale?
Why are candy and magazines always near the register?
What types of food do you think make the store a higher profit?

TIPS

☐ **Make a plan, come with a list.**   Planning your meals ahead of time and using a shopping list saves time, saves money, and encourages healthier eating.

☐ **Compare unit prices.**   Unit prices allow you to compare the price of two packages that may contain a different amount of food. Larger packages often have lower unit prices; however, be sure to consider whether you'll be able to eat the entire amount before it goes bad.

☐ **Look up and look down.**   The most expensive or profitable products are often placed right at eye level. Look on the higher and lower shelves to see if there are cheaper alternatives. Also, watch out for special displays at the end of the aisle. That doesn't mean it's on sale. Sometimes it's just there to get you to buy it.

☐ **Compare brands.**   Store brands and generic products are often identical to name brand products in everything but price. Look at the ingredients list to compare.

☐ **Coupons and sales can be worth it... sometimes.**   Coupons and specials can be a good way to save money—when you use them wisely. Stick to buying bargain items that are already on your list.

☐ **Don't pay for empty calories and low quality ingredients.**   Processed foods often contain ingredients that don't cost the manufacturer a lot of money but they can make a big profit from it. A lot of junk food masquerades as healthy with meaningless front-of-packaging labels like "natural." Remember to check the labels.

© 2024 *Dads Around the Table* Guidebook

How do you think the design or wording on the front of the package tries to influence you to buy it? Do you look at labels on food packages when you are shopping? What do you usually look for? What one item is most useful for you to look at?

☑ *Use this glossary to explore terms typically found on a food label.*

1. **calories**—the energy provided by a food. *Eating more calories than your body uses leads to weight gain.*

2. **carbohydrate**—a nutrient with calories. This is the body's main source of energy. *Carbohydrate-containing foods with fiber provide longer lasting energy.*

3. **fat**—a nutrient that gives a concentrated form of energy, helps absorb other nutrients, and helps build/repair many parts of the body. *High fat foods are also high in calories. Foods labeled low-fat, reduced-fat, or fat-free may have added sugars or other ingredients to make up for the loss of texture or flavor.*

4. **fiber**—a form of carbohydrate that carries water and waste through the body. *Fiber helps you feel full longer, helps lower cholesterol, and controls blood sugar levels.*

5. **GMO-free**—a food without ingredients that had its genetic material artificially manipulated to produce genetically modified organisms. *Some people choose non-GMO foods out of concern for possible unknown effects on the earth and human health.*

6. **gluten-free**—foods without gluten, a type of protein found in some grains (especially wheat). *Some people cannot digest gluten properly or are allergic.*

7. **organic**—foods grown and processed without the use of chemicals. *People may choose organic foods to avoid chemicals for themselves, or to protect farm workers and the earth from chemicals.*

8. **protein**—a nutrient that forms the building blocks of cells, muscles, and tissues. *In addition to animal foods, many plant foods also contain protein.*

9. **sodium, a.k.a. "salt"**—a mineral the body needs in small amounts. *Too much is unhealthy for people with high blood pressure. Processed foods often have a lot.*

10. **sugars**—a form of carbohydrate that gives instant energy. *Processed foods may have unhealthy amounts of added sugars.*

11. **vegan**—foods without any animal products (including eggs or dairy) and made without harming animals.

12. **vitamins and minerals**—compounds the brain and body need in small amounts to function well. *Whole foods and minimally-processed foods contain more vitamins and minerals.*

13. **whole grains**—grains that have not had anything removed in processing. *These have more vitamins, minerals, and fiber than "refined" white grains like white flour and white rice.*

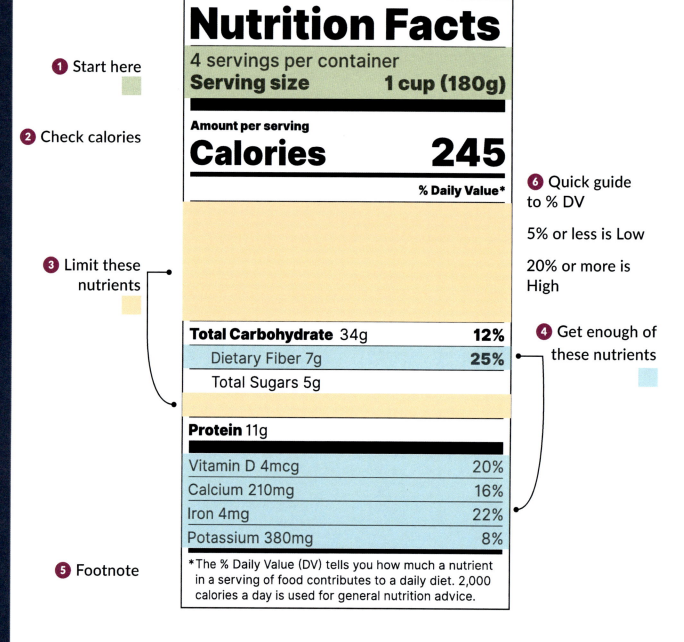

1 Start here

2 Check calories

3 Limit these nutrients

5 Footnote

6 Quick guide to % DV

5% or less is Low

20% or more is High

4 Get enough of these nutrients

Nutrition Facts

4 servings per container
Serving size   1 cup (180g)

Amount per serving
Calories   245

% Daily Value*

Total Carbohydrate 34g	**12%**
Dietary Fiber 7g	**25%**
Total Sugars 5g	
Protein 11g	
Vitamin D 4mcg	20%
Calcium 210mg	16%
Iron 4mg	22%
Potassium 380mg	8%

*The % Daily Value (DV) tells you how much a nutrient in a serving of food contributes to a daily diet. 2,000 calories a day is used for general nutrition advice.

[continues on next page...]

■ What do you look for on a nutrition label?

☑ *There's a lot of information to read; try choosing one or two items to concentrate on at a time.*

1 Check the Serving Size and Servings per Container. Remember the Nutrition Facts label is for one serving. Your package might have more than one serving. If you are eating two servings, then you need to double everything on the label.

2 Calories tells you how much energy you get from eating one serving of this food. Fat-free does not mean calories-free. Items that are fat-free, low-fat, or reduced-fat might have the same amount of calories as the full fat version.

3 The total fat on the label might include monounsaturated and polyunsaturated fats, which are "good fats" that can help lower blood cholesterol. "Zero Trans Fat" foods don't always mean the food is trans-fat-free. The law allows a small amount of trans fat per serving in foods. Read the ingredient list and look for "partially hydrogenated oils" to see if the food has trans fat. Consume foods low in added sugars, saturated fats, and sodium. Cut back on foods higher in these nutrients.

4 Getting enough dietary fiber, vitamins, and minerals can improve overall health and help reduce the risk of some diseases. Choose foods with higher % Daily Value for these nutrients. Fiber also promotes healthy bowel function.

5 The footnote states that the % Daily Value on the nutrition label is based on a 2,000-calorie-diet. The amount of calories and specific nutrients each person needs depends on various factors such as age, body size, and activity levels.

6 % Daily Value on the nutrition labels helps you determine if a serving of that food is high or low in those nutrients. The guide is to choose products that are 5% Daily Value or less for things you want to limit like saturated fat, and sodium. Look for 20% Daily Value or more for things you want to eat more of.

Planning your meals ahead of time saves money and time and encourages healthier eating. It's also a great way to teach your kids about the "real world," so get them involved!

How do I do it?

» Plan your meals for a few days. Using *EatFresh.org,* you can work together, or with your child in mind, to find recipes with ingredients you both enjoy and agree on.

» Make a grocery list that includes all of the ingredients for each dish or recipe. Make sure to check your kitchen for staple ingredients you already have; olive oil, salt, and pepper. You probably don't need to buy everything.

» Sort your grocery list according to the type of food: produce, meat, dairy, and dry goods. Try to guess how much of each thing you need to buy.

» Grocery shop! Save the receipt to help create a budget for the future.

» Review your receipt afterward. Do you see anything surprising?

A Sample Meal Plan and Grocery List:

This Week's Meal	Grocery List
Hearty Egg Burritos *(eatfresh.org/recipe/main-dish-breakfast/ hearty- egg-burritos)*	**Produce** *1 head garlic* *1 bunch green onion* *1 bell pepper-green or red*
	Protein *Eggs*
	Dairy *Low-fat cheddar cheese*
	Grains, Fats and Dry Goods; Canned, Boxed and Packaged *1 package whole wheat tortillas* *Canola Oil* *1 can black beans*

This Week's Meal:

Produce

Protein

Dairy

Grains, Fats and Dry Goods; Canned, Boxed and Packaged

Other

YOU'RE THE CHEF

■ Fresh produce

- » Onions
- » Garlic
- » Mushrooms
- » Broccoli
- » Spinach, kale or collards
- » Lemons

■ Packaged canned goods

- » Whole wheat pasta
- » Brown rice
- » Whole wheat tortillas
- » Canned tomatoes
- » Canned corn
- » Canned beans (any type)

■ Meat/Dairy

- » Ground turkey
- » Cheese (any type)
- » Plain Greek Yogurt

■ Staples

- » Olive oil or Vegetable oil
- » Vinegar
- » Spices, salt, pepper

THINK ABOUT IT

- » What meal could you make using these ingredients? You don't need to use all items!

- » Try to incorporate a protein, a vegetable, and a carbohydrate (grains or starchy vegetables).

- » Think about your favorite cuisines and your cultural traditions.

- » Describe your dish, or draw a picture!

Kids are more likely to try foods they've helped choose and prepare. (Adults too!)

☑ *Review these tips for involving the whole family in meal planning and preparation. Check off any you could do in your home.*

Keep in Mind: Children who have experienced trauma may not follow a typical developmental trend, so your child may need extra support to do these tasks.

Preschoolers

- » Spread nut butter or cream cheese on bread
- » Help wash veggies and fruit
- » Help select foods at the grocery store
- » Carry unbreakable items to and from table
- » Serve themselves at the table (with help)
- » Pour liquids into batters (you measure)
- » Stir or mix the batter, or other wet or dry ingredients
- » Knead bread dough; press cookie cutters into dough or bread
- » Use a damp sponge to wipe counters, tables, and chairs after eating

Remember: Preschoolers want to learn and explore what you are exploring. While they may not eat the food they help prepare, touching, smelling, talking about the food, and seeing others eat it will help them learn to try new things.

Elementary school kids

- » Tell other family members what's in a recipe or why foods are healthy
- » Practice cutting softer ingredients with a butter knife, strong plastic knife, or a paring knife (supervise when using sharp knives)
- » Grate or mash soft fruits, veggies, and beans; juice lemons or limes; crack eggs
- » Serve themselves and others at the table
- » Begin to read recipes and measure with cups and spoons
- » Begin to learn stovetop and oven basics (with supervision)
- » Set/clear the table; wash, dry, and put away dishes

Remember: Encourage kids to be "produce pickers" by choosing fruits and veggies at the store. Try reintroducing foods they might not have liked when they were younger. As they get older, they are more likely to eat stronger flavored foods.

Older kids, teens, and adults

- » Find and choose recipes; prepare a whole meal; help meal plan
- » Help grocery shopping, making lists & budget
- » Set/clear table, wash, dry, and put away dishes
- » Read food labels for ingredients, nutrients, and health claims
- » Chop ingredients with a knife (supervise as needed)
- » Use kitchen appliances

Remember: Youth are naturally curious about cooking and like to be creative. This may seem like a hassle at times, but it means they're paying attention to food—which is healthy in the long run!

Anyone

- » Say "grace" or offer thanks for a meal
- » Decorate or make the table look special
- » Help clean up

MORE ABOUT COOKING & NUTRITION

■ Why is it important to practice good food safety?

✅ *Follow these tips to create a safer kitchen.*

1. Keep food preparation surfaces (cutting boards, counters, etc.) clean, since these are breeding grounds for bacteria.

   » If you use a cutting board and knife to cut raw meat, fish or poultry, be sure to clean and sanitize the surface before using it again. Some people keep two cutting boards: one for raw foods and one for ready-to-eat foods.

2. Cook foods thoroughly.

   » When meat is exposed to air, bacteria immediately begins to develop. For that reason, hamburgers must always be cooked through, while a steak is safe to eat medium rare.

   » To be safe, invest in a meat thermometer and test the meat for doneness.

3. Store raw meat and uncooked food on a lower shelf of your refrigerator.

   » Also, keep eggs off the door and near the back where temperatures remain the coldest.

   » Your refrigerator should be kept at 40° F or less.

4. Refrigerate prepared foods within two hours of cooking or buying them.

   » Properly refrigerated food can be eaten for 3-5 days. When in doubt, throw it out!

5. There are four ways to safely defrost foods:

   » Overnight in the refrigerator.

   » In a bowl of cold water, with the water changed every 30 minutes.

   » In the microwave.

   » During cooking.

   Note: It is NEVER safe to leave frozen meat out on the countertop to defrost.

6. To ensure you have clean hands, wash them in hot, soapy water for at least 20 seconds. When teaching kids, have them sing the ABCs while washing.

7. When you wash dishes, either use an automatic dishwasher or wash them in the sink and allow to air dry.

   » Damp dish towels can harbor bacteria.

What can go wrong if you don't read a recipe well?

It's easy to miss details in a recipe. Perhaps you invent something new...
or have to throw out your dinner!

Smoothies

Prep Time: 5 min   Cook Time: 0 min   Yield: 2 servings

Ingredients:

» 4 frozen strawberries

» 1 cup low-fat plain yogurt

» ½ cup 100% orange juice

» 1 banana, cut into chunks

» 4 ice cubes

Directions:

» Place all ingredients in a blender.

» Cover and process until smooth.

Per 1 Cup Serving: 150 calories, 2g total fat (1g sat),
30g carb, 2g fiber, 65mg sodium

1. Read the recipe well before starting.
   » Make sure you have all the items you need and enough time for the recipe.
   » When an ingredient is optional, you don't have to use it unless you want to.
   » If necessary, preheat the oven while you prepare.

2. Prepare ingredients for the recipe.
   » If a recipe calls for chopped onion, for example, do the chopping now. You might also need to bring ingredients to room temperature, melt them, or chill them before starting.
   » To learn about ingredient substitutions, go to the "Discover Foods" tab of eatfresh.org.

3. Measure carefully.
   » It helps to know abbreviations: **c.** = cup, **T.** or **tbsp**. = tablespoon, **t.** or **tsp**. = teaspoon. It's also helpful to know measurement shortcuts. For example:
   » 4 Tablespoons = ¼ cup
   » 3 teaspoons = 1 Tablespoon

4. Pay attention to the order of the steps.

5. If you make any changes to your recipe as you cook, make a note. That way you can prepare the dish exactly the same way next time—or not!

Do you know common measurement abbreviations, tools, and equivalents? These are helpful in reading and understanding recipes.

■ Recognize the abbreviations

» Cup: c.

» Fluid ounce: fl oz.

» Gallon: g or gal.

» Gram: g.

» Kilogram: kg.

» Milliliter: ml.

» Ounce: oz.

» Pound: lb.

» Quart: q or qt.

» Teaspoon: t or tsp.

» Tablespoon: T or tbsp.

■ Choose the correct tool

» Use measuring spoons for small amounts of liquid or dry ingredients.

» Use liquid measuring cups for larger amounts of liquids.

» Use dry measuring cups for larger amounts of solid or semisolid ingredients like flour, rice, or sugar.

» Recipes sometime give amounts in weight.

» Non-liquid packaged products sometimes show how much they weigh on the label. Don't confuse liquid ounces with dry ounces.

■ Measure accurate equivalents

» 3 tsp = 1 tbsp

» 4 tbsp = 1/4 cup

» 8 tbsp = 1/2 cup

» 16 tbsp = 1 cup

» 4 cups = 1 quart

» 4 quarts = 1 gallon

» 1 pound = 16 ounces (dry weight)

» 1 cup = 8 ounces (liquids only)

■ Measuring Dry Ingredients

1. Scoop the ingredient into the dry measuring cup or spoon.

2. Use the back of a utensil to smooth the top.

■ Measuring Liquid Ingredients

1. Fill the liquid measuring cup up to the line.

2. Place it on a level surface to confirm measurement.

3. Bend down so you are at eye-level with the measurement to read it accurately.

[continues on next page...]

1 TSP + 1 TSP + 1 TSP = 1 TBSP

1 TBSP + 1 TBSP + 1 TBSP + 1 TBSP + 1 TBSP + 1 TBSP + 1 TBSP + 1 TBSP = ½ CUP

1 CUP — 8 OUNCES

1 POUND = 16 OUNCES

1 CUP + 1 CUP + 1 CUP + 1 CUP = 1 QUART

1 QUART + 1 QUART + 1 QUART + 1 QUART = 1 GALLON

How can you eat well when you're low on time and energy? Here are some tips.

» **Learn how to chop vegetables quickly and efficiently.** Most people chop onions slowly. Take a few minutes to learn to do it quickly.

» **Pre-chop vegetables** on the weekend or in the morning to cut down on time spent on evening prep. Or, chop more veggies than you need so you are preparing for the next meal. Put them in a reusable container or plastic bag to store in the refrigerator or freezer.

» **Use a sharp knife.** Dull knives are dangerous and require much more energy to use. Also, avoid using a small knife for larger foods.

» **Learn to eyeball common measurements;** know what one cup of chopped veggies looks like on a cutting board or a teaspoon of a spice in the palm of your hand. In most cases, it's not essential to be exact (baking is an exception).

» **Get a head start.** In the morning, lay out any pots or pans you'll need in the evening. If your veggies are already chopped and your pots laid out, you are more likely to cook.

» **Enlist helpers.** Have kids in the house? Ask them to wipe and set the table, wash the veggies, or help gather the ingredients.

» **Try a different tool.** Slow cookers (crock-pots) and rice cookers are great time savers and often available for a few dollars at second-hand stores.

» **Double the yield.** Cook extra chicken one night that can be made into a few different meals like tacos or soup, or used as a salad topper.

» **Keep prepped veggies in the freezer.** Always have frozen vegetables in the freezer—no need to wash or chop!

TRY IT!

Visit: bit.ly/chop-onion for a chopping demonstration.

Which color do you eat the most?

Different colored fruits and vegetables are full of different nutrients. How can you add variety throughout your day?

Green

- » Lower your chance of getting cancer
- » Keep your eyes healthy
- » Keep your bones and teeth strong

Spinach, celery, green beans, broccoli, cabbage, bok choy, cucumbers, asparagus, kale, artichokes, honeydew, green grapes, green apples, limes, avocados

Yellow and Orange

- » Keep your heart healthy
- » Keep your eyes healthy
- » Lower your chance of getting cancer
- » Keep you from catching colds

Carrots, sweet potatoes, yellow peppers, pumpkins, pineapple, papayas, cantaloupe, tangerines, mangoes, oranges, lemons, peaches

Red

- » Keep your heart healthy
- » Keep your bladder healthy
- » Keep your memory strong
- » Lower your chance of getting cancer

Tomatoes, red peppers, strawberries, cherries, watermelon, red onion, red apples, beets

Blue and Purple

- » Stay healthy as you age
- » Keep your bladder healthy
- » Keep your memory strong
- » Lower your chance of getting cancer

Eggplant, raisins, blueberries, blackberries, purple grapes, purple cabbage

White/Brown

- » Keep your heart healthy
- » Have good cholesterol levels
- » Lower your chance of getting cancer

Onion, green onion, cauliflower, chives, mushrooms, ginger, garlic, jicama, fennel

STORING YOUR PRODUCE

Here are some tips to store your produce to make it last longer.

■ 1. Keep your produce whole.

» Don't even rip the stem out of an apple until you eat it. As soon as you start pulling fruits and vegetables apart, you've broken cells and given a surface for microorganisms to grow. Mold proliferates rapidly and contaminates everything nearby, so toss any spoiled produce immediately.

■ 2. Keep incompatible fruits and veggies separate.

» You might have heard that to speed-ripen a peach, you put it in a closed paper bag with a ripe banana. Some fruits (like bananas) give off high levels of ethylene—an odorless, colorless gas that speeds up ripening of nearby ethylene-sensitive produce. "Gas releasers" are one of the main causes of premature decay. One bad apple really can spoil the whole bunch. Use our quick reference guide to the right and keep all "gas releasers" (the first two groups) separate from ethylene-sensitive produce (the third group).

■ 3. Know what to refrigerate and what to eat first.

» The main way to lengthen shelf life of produce is by using cold temperatures to slow food's respiration, or 'breathing' process, so less ethylene gas is emitted and the ripening process is slowed. The warmer the temperature, the faster the rate of respiration, which is why refrigeration is critical for most produce. But while you want to slow it down, you don't want to stop the breathing all together. The worst thing to do is seal fruits and vegetables in an airtight bag, because you'll suffocate them and speed up decay.

» A big part of correct storage is knowing what to refrigerate. Cold-sensitive fruits and veggies lose flavor and moisture at low temperatures. Store them on the counter, not the fridge. Once they're fully ripe, you can refrigerate them to help them last, but for best flavor, return them to room temp. Never refrigerate potatoes, onions, winter squash, or garlic. Keep them in a cool, dry, dark place, and they can last up to a month or more. Light and heat will cause them to sprout. But separate them so their flavors and smells don't migrate.

» New innovations: Some products you can purchase absorb ethylene and can be dropped into a crisper with vegetables. A variety of produce bags both absorb ethylene and create an atmosphere that inhibits respiration.

Refrigerate these "gas releasers"

Apples

Apricots

Cantaloupe

Figs

Honeydew

Don't refrigerate these "gas releasers"

Avocados

Bananas, unripe

Nectarines

Peaches

Pears

Plums

Tomatoes

Store these away from ALL "gas releasers"

Bananas, ripe

Broccoli

Brussels sprouts

Cabbage

Carrots

Cauliflower

Cucumbers

Eggplant

Lettuce and other leafy greens

Parsley

Peas

Peppers

Squash

Sweet potatoes

Watermelon

[continues on next page...]

▪ 4. Know what to eat first.

» Eat more perishable items first and save the longer-lasting produce for later in the week. Use this quick guide to help you decide what to eat first. The timing suggestions are for ready-to-eat produce, so allow extra days for ripening if you're buying not-quite-ripe fruits or vegetables.

▪ 5. Storage starts with the shopping bag.

» Many people don't realize storage starts even before the shopping bag makes it home. Shop for less perishable items like potatoes, onions, and melons first and keep heavier items on the bottom of the bag. Shop for more perishable items like berries and broccoli last so they don't get warm while you shop (and emit more ethylene gas, which will ripen them faster). Get the produce home quickly and into a dark cool place or into your refrigerator if you have one. The earlier you shop at the farmer's market the fresher the produce will be, the less time it has spent outside in warm temperatures, and the longer it will last at home.

▪ 6. Have a backup plan.

» If you find yourself with more ripe produce than you can eat, have a strategy for how to use it up quickly. Use a crock pot to make an easy potful of soup with any leftover vegetables. Get creative and try a new recipe, like a big pie for your neighbor or a pot of tomato sauce to freeze in individual packages.

» Some fruits and vegetables can be stored in the freezer for using later. Fruits like berries are fine to freeze as-is. Fruits that tend to brown easily, like apples or peaches, should be soaked in an acidic juice before freezing to help them maintain their color.

» Most vegetables need to be blanched before freezing, which involves submerging them briefly in boiling water or steaming to destroy the enzymes that cause spoiling. Onions, peppers, and herbs do not need to be blanched. Squash, sweet potatoes, and pumpkin should be fully cooked before freezing. All other vegetables should be blanched.

» The amount of time you should leave each variety of vegetable submerged in boiling water varies. Use the internet or a library book to look up instructions.

Thank you to Heart of the City Farmer's Market, San Francisco California, and Vegetarian Times for this information.

Eat first (within 1-3 days)
Artichokes
Asparagus
Avocados
Bananas
Broccoli
Cherries
Corn
Green beans
Mushrooms
Strawberries

Eat second (within 4-6 days)
Cucumbers
Eggplant
Grapes
Lettuce
Limes
Zucchini

Eat third (within 6-8 days)
Apricots
Bell peppers
Blueberries
Brussels sprouts
Cauliflower
Leeks
Oranges
Peaches
Pears
Plums
Spinach
Tomatoes

Eat last (longest lasting)
Apples
Cabbage
Celery
Garlic
Onions
Potatoes
Winter squash

TRY-AT-HOME ACTIVITIES

Practicing mindfulness techniques can help us be present and better handle moments when we are feeling overwhelmed or stuck. You can do them before bedtime, before mealtimes, or any time you need them. Keep these activities near your bed, in the kitchen, or somewhere accessible. Find one that you like to do regularly and share it with your kids.

5-4-3-2-1

- Put your feet flat on the ground and take a breath in and out through your nose
  Silently, to yourself name:
  - » 5 things you can see in the room
  - » 4 things you can hear in the room
  - » 3 sensations you feel in your body
  - » 2 things you can smell
- Finally, [pick one]
  - » 1 thing for which you are grateful
  - » 1 thing that inspires you
  - » 1 person you appreciate
  - » 1 wish for the world
  - » 1 hope or dream for yourself

Self-Holding Exercise

- » Get into a comfortable position either seated or lying down.
- » Place one hand on your forehead. Place the other hand on your heart.
- » Gently place your attention on the area between your two hands, the area inside yourself between your head and heart.
- » Just feel what goes on in the area between your hands.
- » Gently breathe in and out.
- » Do this for as long as you can or need to in order to feel yourself shift into a more relaxed state.

Soup Bowl Breathing

» Think of your favorite soup.

» Gently cup your hands like you are holding your favorite soup. You can also just put your hands down in your lap. Sit up tall, like your spine was made of a stack of pennies, with both feet on the floor. Close your eyes or glance down.

» Imagine breathing in through your nose like you are smelling a delicious bowl of soup, and breathing out like you are blowing on it to cool down—careful so as not to splash soup everywhere!

» Breathe in for four seconds. Breathe out for eight seconds. Repeat three times.

Box Breathing

Try this one if you need to be more alert.

» Place feet flat on the ground or lie down. Roll back shoulders.

» Place hand on belly.

» Take a deep breath in through your nose for 4 counts, allowing your belly to expand.

» Hold the breath for 4 counts.

» Exhale deeply through the mouth for 4 counts, contracting belly.

» Hold for 4 counts.

» Repeat 4 times.

8-5-2-1 Countdown Shake-Out

1. Place feet shoulder distance apart. Softly bend the knees. Shake out each limb (left hand, right hand, left food, right food), counting down from 8..., then 5..., 2.., and 1.

2. Left hand shake - "8,7,6,5,4,3,2,1"

3. Right hand shake - "8,7,6,5,4,3,2,1"

4. Left foot shake - "8,7,6,5,4,3,2,1"

5. Right foot shake - "8,7,6,5,4,3,2,1"

Repeat the sequence, counting down from 5, then 2, then 1.

Belly Massage

1. Place one hand or fist above the right hip and a little inwards towards the belly button.

2. Using the whole palm and applying light or medium pressure, slide the hand up along the right side, across the top of the belly, and then down the left side.

3. Continue sliding across the bottom and repeat up, across, down, across.

» This movement may help with indigestion, cramping, gas, and constipation.

» This technique can be done with two fingers and light pressure for babies or small children.

Butterfly Tapping

1. Cross your wrists at chest height like a butterfly.
2. Rhythmically tap your upper chest from side to side, deciding how firm or fast feels right for you. Remember to keep your elbows soft.
3. Count down from 10 to 1.

Pressure Point Tapping

Try these three levels of pressure:

» **Softest** (Snowflake Taps): Fluttering fingers

» **Medium** (Raindrop Taps): Firmer finger taps

» **Firm** (Thunder Taps): Knuckles

1. Using both hands, start with the snowflake tap at the crown of your head.
2. Tap gently at the crown of the head, the eyebrows, temples, and the top of the cheek.
3. With one hand, tap the upper lip, above chin/under the lower lip.
4. Return to two hands, tapping under the collarbones, then below the armpit (this may be easier with the arms crossed). Finally, with your palms facing up, tap the inside of your wrists.
5. Now repeat these same areas with raindrop taps, then with thunder taps. Experiment and find the pressure that feels right for you.

   Reminder: Notice your breath and any tension you may be holding. Let go as you move through the pressure points.

TABLE TALK

■ Conversation

Stir up an interesting conversation with your family using these questions in the car, at home, via text, or at the table. Let everyone pick a question they want to answer first. Then others can answer if they wish. Don't force anyone to answer a question if they don't want to.

■ For all ages

1. If you could be anyone in the world for a day, who would it be and why?

2. What is something you want to learn that they don't teach you in school?

3. What are three things you learned in school today?

4. If you could grow up to be famous, what would you want to be famous for?

5. What do you like most about yourself?

6. What is the most unusual thing you have ever eaten?

7. Finish this sentence: I am really good at……

8. If you could have any talent, what would it be and why?

9. If you could invent something that would make life easier for people, what would it be?

10. If you could ask your favorite animal a question, what would you ask?

11. If you could make any food in the world, what would you make?

12. If you could change one rule, what would you change?

13. If you could have special powers, what powers would you want to have and why?

14. What is the funniest thing you have ever seen?

15. What is one thing you wish adults understood better about being your age?

16. What is one thing you wish you understood better about adults and why?

17. What is one thing people don't know about you that you wish they knew?

18. What kind of food best describes your personality?

For ages 12+

1. What is the scariest thing about becoming an adult?

2. Why do you think people give up on their dreams?

3. What is your most important goal right now?

4. What is one lesson that you had to learn the hard way and what did you learn?

5. What are your three best and worst qualities?

6. If you could teach any class, what would it be and why?

7. What is your biggest accomplishment and why?

8. What are three traits you look for in a friend?

9. Would you rather have a job with average pay you love or a job with great pay you dislike? Why?

10. What makes you happy and why?

11. What is one thing you are afraid of and why?

12. Do you consider yourself an optimist or a pessimist? Why?

13. Who is someone that you admire and why?

14. What is an essential life skill you need in order to live on your own?

15. What is one goal you want to achieve in the next year?

16. If you could meet one historical figure, living or dead, who would it be and why?

17. If you had 5 minutes to meet with the U.S. President, what would you say?

18. What is one thing people don't know about you that you wish they knew?

■ Activity: Be the Chef!

Directions: On pages 59 and 60 have your child draw their favorite foods as a meal or design a balanced MyPlate meal they would like to have.

Encourage them to be as creative and colorful as possible. (You can suggest they draw inspiration from their favorite cuisines, cultural traditions, holidays, or a meal that they enjoy.)

1. You can ask: What healthy foods would be on this plate? What "fun" foods would be on this plate?

2. When they are finished drawing, ask them about their meal:
   » Why did you choose this meal?
   » What is your favorite ingredient in this meal? Why?
   » Do you have a memory of this meal that you would like to share?
   » How do you feel when you eat this meal?
   » What colors are in this meal?
   » Describe the flavors of this meal, either real or imaginary.

3. Optional: Make your child's meal.
   » Work together to create an ingredient list and make the meal together.
   » Enjoy!

☑ *Draw your favorite meal or a meal you would like to have.*

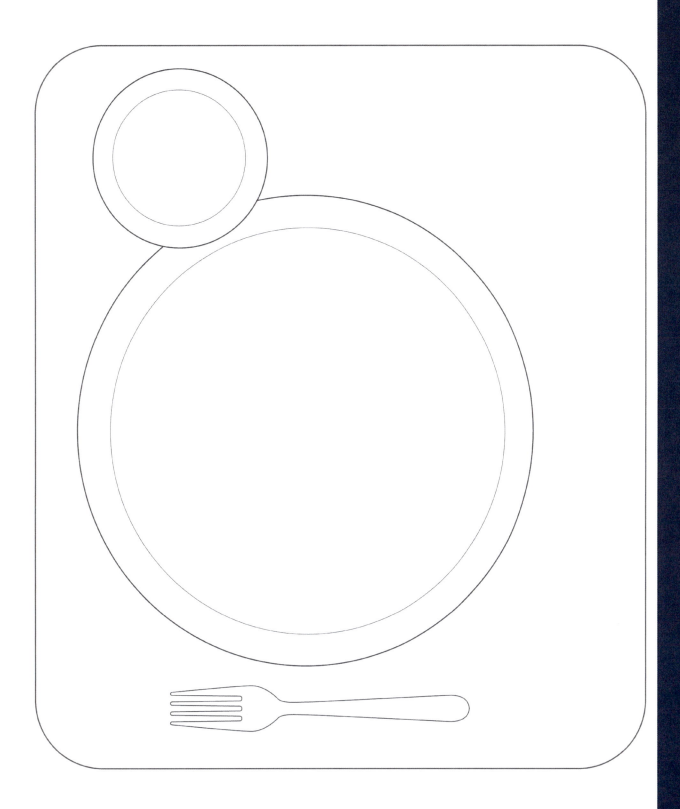

☑ *Draw or write in some foods that fit each category.*

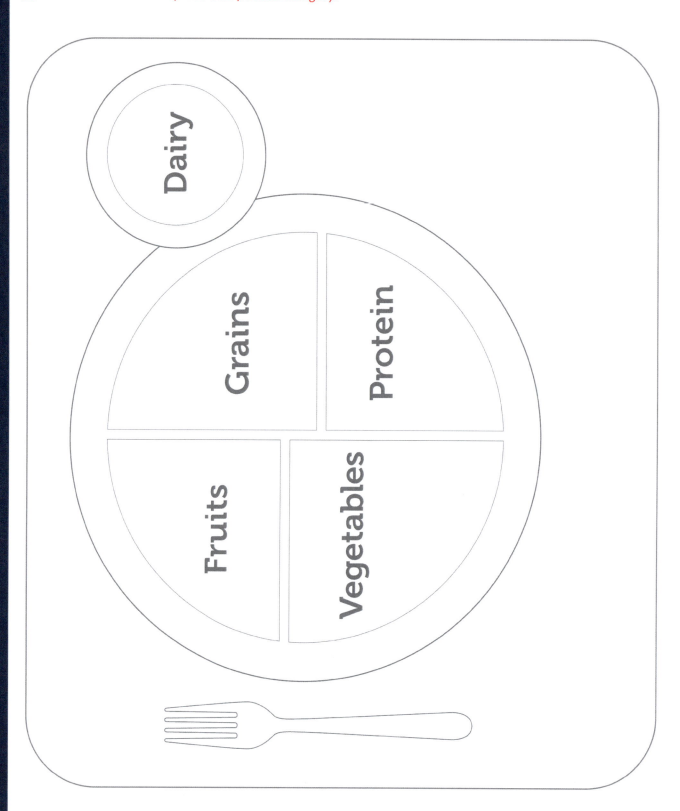

Use these questions as a way for you and your child to learn about each other's food choices/preferences and create a mutual connection. Take turns interviewing each other and let your child interview you first.

1. *What is one food you associate with your childhood? Why?*

2. *What is most important to you about food?*

3. *What is your favorite comfort food—something you crave when you are stressed or emotional? Why?*

4. *What is a food that you have always wanted to try but haven't yet?*

5. *How did you learn about food and cooking? Who did you learn from?*

6. *Describe a favorite food memory. What made that moment special?*

7. *What are some foods that celebrate your culture?*

8. *What are your favorite and least favorite food textures?*

9. *How have your eating habits changed throughout your life?*

10. *What is something you dislike eating that other people love?*

■ _____'s _____ and _____ Oven-Baked Omelette
    (name someone special)   *(vegetable)*   *(another vegetable)*

Serves 6

■ Directions

1. Preheat the oven to 350°F.

2. In a big bowl, whisk 8 eggs with ½ cup of _____.
   (milk or non-dairy alternative)

3. Heat 2 tablespoons of butter or oil in a large oven-proof skillet over medium heat. Then add 1–2 cups of chopped _____.
   (your chosen vegetables)

4. When the vegetables are tender, add 1 teaspoon _____.
   (dried herbs or spices)

5. Pour the egg mixture over the other ingredients in the skillet. Allow to cook, without stirring, for 1–2 minutes.

6. Sprinkle with a handful of crumbled _____,
   (cheese)

7. Bake in the oven for 15–20 minutes or until the center is just firm.

8. Remove the omelette from the oven and let cool a little before slicing and serving.

■ Tip: If you don't have an oven-proof skillet, oil or butter the bottom of a baking pan. Spread vegetable mixture on the bottom and pour in beaten eggs before baking.

IDEA BANK

Vegetables	Herbs & Spices	Cheese
spinach	basil	Parmesan or Romano
squash	oregano	cheddar
mushrooms	thyme	mozzarella
Swiss chard	parsley	Swiss cheese
asparagus	tarragon	Jack cheese
peas	chile powder	
corn kernels	turmeric	
onion	cilantro	
broccoli		
bell pepper		

■ _____'s Dinner Salad with _____ and _____

(name someone special)   (salad greens)   (protein or whole grain)

Serves 6

■ Directions

1. In a giant bowl, whisk together ⅓ cup olive oil with 3 tablespoons_____

    (acid, like vinegar, lemon)

    ,

    1 teaspoon_____, and a pinch of salt.

    (dried spices or herbs)

2. To the bowl, add up to 2 cups each of_____,

    (crunchy raw vegetables)

    _____ , _____,

    (chosen cooked protein or whole grain)   (something juicy, chopped)

    and_____. Toss them in the dressing. Taste a piece of lettuce and

    (another fruit or vegetable)

    adjust seasonings or acid.

3. Add about 6 cups of_____, chopped or torn into bite-sized pieces.

    (chosen salad greens)

4. Add _____ .

    (up to 1 cup fun addition)

5. Toss everything really well to coat with the dressing. Serve at room temperature.

IDEA BANK

Acids
fresh citrus juice
apple cider vinegar
balsamic vinegar
wine vinegar
rice vinegar (with soy sauce)

Herbs and Spices
basil
oregano
thyme
parsley
mint
ginger
chile flakes
mustard
black pepper

Raw Vegetables
chopped bell peppers
chopped or shredded carrots
sliced avocado

sliced cucumbers
chopped celery
shaved fennel

Proteins & Whole Grains
cooked chicken, turkey, or
    steak
cooked shrimp
canned tuna or salmon*
cubed marinated tofu
sliced hard-boiled egg
cooked chickpeas, kidney
    beans
cooked quinoa
cooked whole grain pasta
cooked wild rice, brown or red
    rice
*Drain canned fish

Something Juicy
tomatoes
corn kernels

orange or grapefruit segments
sliced plums or peaches
sliced apples or pears
chunks of mango or pineapple

Salad Greens
spinach
lettuce
cabbage
arugula
kale

Fun additions
pitted olives
nuts or seeds
sliced or shredded cheese
tortilla strips or croutons
dried fruit such as raisins,
    cranberries, cherries

■ Fried _____ with _____ and _____
    (whole grain)   *(protein)*   *(vegetable or fruit)*

Serves 4

■ Directions

1. Heat a big skillet over high heat, then add 2 tablespoons vegetable oil (not olive).

2. When the oil is hot, turn down the heat to medium, and add a handful of some
   chopped _____.
                (onion, garlic, or shallot)

3. Stir in a cup of _____.
                        (your chosen protein)

4. When the protein is cooked through, remove from pan and set aside. Add 1 tbsp.
   vegetable oil and 2 cups chopped _____. Keep stirring.
                                            (veggies, at least 2 kinds)

5. Add 2 cups of cold cooked_____, ½ cup of _____
                                  (your chosen whole grain)   *(fun addition *option)*
   and a few tablespoons of _____.
                                  (salty or spicy sauce)

6. Stir everything until all the ingredients are heated through and steaming.

7. Taste and adjust the seasonings. Serve hot.

IDEA BANK

Proteins
peeled shrimp
chopped chicken breast
chopped ham
lean ground beef, turkey
tofu, tempeh, or seitan
eggs, beaten

Whole Grains
brown rice
quinoa
barley
farro
whole wheat couscous

Vegetables
celery
zucchini
carrots
peas
bell peppers
broccoli or cauliflower
scallions
mushrooms
cabbage
asparagus
green beans

Fun Additions
peanuts, walnuts, cashews
chopped mango, pineapple
sesame seeds

Salty or Spicy Sauces
soy sauce
teriyaki sauce
fish sauce
sweet chile sauce
hot sauce

■ Cheesy Baked Pasta with _____ with _____
    (greens)   *(extras)*

Serves 4

■ Directions

1. Preheat oven to 400° F. Grease a baking dish.

2. Boil a large pot of salted water. Add 1 pound of whole grain _____
    (pasta)

    and cook until it's almost, but not quite, done (still a little firm, also known as al dente).

3. While the pasta cooks, grate 8 oz. of _____ into a large bowl.
    (cheese)

    Add a cup of milk and a teaspoon of _____
    (herbs and spices)

4. Fold in 2 cups of chopped _____ and some _____ .
    (greens)   *(toppings)*

5. If you'd like, sprinkle some _____ over the top.
    (extras)

6. Drain the pasta and mix with the other ingredients. Then pour the whole thing into your
    baking dish. Bake for 15 minutes or until golden brown on top.

IDEA BANK

Pasta (try whole wheat)
macaroni
spaghetti
shells
penne
rice stick noodles
egg noodles

Cheese
Parmesan
cheddar
Monterey Jack
Gruyère, mozzarella, or Swiss

Herbs and Spices
dried or fresh oregano
fresh basil
fresh parsley

chile powder
garlic powder
mustard

Greens (raw or cooked)
cooked spinach
Swiss chard
kale
arugula
collards

Extras
cooked chicken, ham, or
    sausage
caramelized onions
sautéed mushrooms
chopped sun-dried tomatoes
chopped pitted olives

corn
frozen peas
cooked broccoli or cauliflower

Toppings
bread crumbs or croutons
crispy onions
crushed crackers or chips
more shredded cheese

RECIPES

RECIPE MATRIX

RECIPE	One-Pot/One Bowl	Microwave	Flavor with Herbs & Spices	Lunch on the Go	Quick Snacks	Entrees with Meat	Meatless Entrees	No Cook	Prep Ahead
Egg Burritos				X			X		
Spiced Trail Mix	X				X			X	X
Spring Spread	X				X			X	
Green Smoothie	X				X			X	
One Mug Omelette	X	X			X		X		
Black Bean and Vegetable Tostadas							X		X
Southwest Baked Potato		X					X		X
Ground Chicken Lettuce Wraps						X			X
Pita Pizzas				X	X		X		X

Ready In 30 min.

Serves 4

It's easy to find burritos in the frozen foods case at your grocery store or at fast food restaurants. But you can make your own with a lot more flavor and nutrients. These egg burritos can be frozen and reheated for breakfast, dinner, or any time you need a balanced meal on the go.

Ingredients

3 green onions, *sliced*	4 large eggs
1 red or green bell pepper, *diced small*	¼ c. cilantro, *chopped* (optional)
1 clove garlic, *minced*	¾ tsp. ground cumin, *divided*
1 (15.5-oz) can no-salt added black beans, *drained and rinsed*	¼ tsp. ground black pepper
	4 (8-inch) whole wheat flour tortillas
2 tsp. oil, *divided*	½ c. low-fat cheddar cheese, *grated*

❋ **Notes:** *If you double the recipe, do not double cumin. Also, when a recipe says "divided" or "separated," it means you will use that ingredient in more than one place in the dish, rather than all at once.*

Directions

1. Heat oil in a medium skillet over medium heat. Add beans, green onions, bell pepper, and garlic. Cook until peppers are soft, about 3 minutes. Add ½ tsp. ground cumin and black pepper. Transfer mixture to a bowl.

2. In a small bowl, crack eggs. Add remaining ¼ tsp. cumin. Beat mixture lightly with a fork.

3. Wipe out skillet with a paper towel. Heat 1 tsp oil on medium-low. Add egg mixture. Cook, stirring occasionally, until eggs are as firm as you like. If using cilantro, add now.

4. Spoon egg mixture into the center of each tortilla, dividing evenly. Add beans and veggies. Sprinkle cheese on top.

5. Fold tortilla over mixture and serve.

❋ **Tips:** *Burritos can be frozen for up to one week. Wrap tightly in plastic wrap, cover with aluminum foil, and freeze. To reheat, remove foil and plastic. Microwave 1 ½ – 2 minutes, turning as needed. Or, remove plastic wrap and re-cover in aluminum foil. Heat in a toaster oven or regular oven at 300° F for about 6 minutes.*

Nutrition Info *per 1 burrito*

Total calories: 330
Carbohydrates: 45 g
Total fat: 9 g
Saturated fat: 1 g
Protein: 20 g
Fiber: 9 g
Sodium: 510 mg

Authors: Leah's Pantry

SPICED TRAIL MIX

In order to keep them low-cost and last long on the shelf, processed snack foods often contain preservatives or other ingredients you would never use at home. These ingredients may also negatively your health. Mix up a batch of this trail mix to pack as a snack. Just a little bit is enough to satisfy cravings for sweet, salt, and crunch without a lot of junk.

Ingredients

- 1 c. peanuts or other nuts
- 1 c. raisins or other dried fruit
- 1 c. sunflower or pumpkin seeds, *raw or roasted*
- 1 c. bite-sized pretzels, dry low sugar cereal, or small crackers
- 1 tbsp. paprika and/or cinnamon
- Salt, *to taste*
- 1 c. dried shredded coconut, chocolate chips, or additional dried fruit (optional)

Directions

1. Toss all ingredients well and enjoy.

❋ **Tip:** *Look for cereals with less than 6g of sugar per serving.*

Nutrition Info *per ¼ cup serving*

Total calories: 196
Carbohydrates: 19 g
Total fat: 13 g
Saturated fat: 2 g
Protein: 6 g
Fiber: 4 g
Sodium: 113 mg

Authors: Leah's Pantry

Ready In 10 min.   **Serves** 4

This spread makes a great snack, sandwich filling, or dip. It's also way more nutritious than packaged dips and spreads thanks to several colors of fresh vegetables. Note that the smaller you chop or grate the vegetables, the more the flavors blend together— and might make it more enticing to picky eaters.

Ingredients

4   oz. low-fat cream cheese, *whipped or softened*
½   carrot, *grated*
½   red bell pepper, *finely diced*
2   green onions, *finely chopped*

1   tsp. freshly squeezed lemon or lime juice
1   tbsp. fresh herbs, *chopped* (see tip)
Serve with: whole grain crackers, tortillas, bagels, celery sticks, or cucumber slices

Directions

1. Mix all ingredients with a rubber spatula until creamy.

2. Use as a spread for breads, crackers, or on vegetables.

✳ *Tip: This is a great way to use up leftover herbs (such as dill, thyme, oregano, basil) and vegetables.*

Nutrition Info *2 tbsp. serving*

Total calories: 61
Carbohydrates: 3 g
Total fat: 4 g
Saturated fat: 3 g
Protein: 2 g
Fiber: <1 g
Sodium: 106 mg

Authors: Leah's Pantry

GREEN SMOOTHIE

Ready In 5 min. **Serves** 2

In recent years, bottled juices and smoothies have become more popular. These can be expensive though, and often contain just as much sugar as soft drinks! This smoothie is an inexpensive, nutrient-packed alternative you can make yourself. It's also a great way to add greens to your diet, even if you don't love their flavor. Use at least one kind of frozen fruit to make this cold, thick and creamy.

Ingredients

2   large handful raw greens such as spinach or kale (about 1 c.)
1   medium banana

2   c. other fresh or frozen fruit, *chopped*
2   c. milk or milk substitute

Directions

1. Place all ingredients in a blender in the order listed.

2. Blend until smooth and creamy. Add a little water if desired for a thinner smoothie.

3. Serve immediately.

❊ **Tip:** *Yellow, green, or orange fruits make this smoothie a pretty color while reds and purples might make it look a little darker or grayer. Regardless, any color fruit tastes delicious!*

Nutrition Info *per 2 cup serving*

Total calories: 218
Carbohydrates: 45 g
Total fat: 1.5 g
Saturated fat: <1 g
Protein: 10 g
Fiber: 6 g
Sodium: 129 mg

Authors: Leah's Pantry

Ready In 5 min. | **Serves** 1

Ingredients

Oil for greasing
1 egg
2 tbsp. milk, low fat or 2 tbsp. water

Salt, to taste
Black pepper, to taste

✳ **Notes:** *You may need to cook this recipe for more or less time depending on your microwave.*

Directions

1. Grease a mug with cooking spray, or butter.

2. *In a bowl, use a fork to beat the egg, milk or water, salt, and pepper.*

3. *Mix in your choice of additions.*

4. *Pour the mixture into the mug.*

5. *Microwave for 1 minute. Check that egg is fully cooked and not wet. If it's still wet, microwave for an additional 30-60 seconds.*

✳ **Tip:** *Add more color and fiber with vegetables such as: diced onion, bell pepper, tomatoes, cooked broccoli, fresh or frozen spinach.*

Nutrition Info *per 1 cup serving*

Total calories: 104
Carbohydrates: 2 g
Total fat: 7 g
Saturated fat: 2 g
Protein: 7 g
Sodium: 85 mg

Authors: Leah's Pantry

BLACK BEAN AND VEGETABLE TOSTADAS

Ready In 25 min. **Serves** 5

Beans and vegetables on a crispy tortilla combine to be a filling, satisfying, and nourishing meal. It is almost like a fast food taco except you know exactly what you put into it.

Ingredients

1   tbsp. oil, *separated*
¼   c. chopped onion
1   small red bell pepper, *diced*
1   c. canned, defrosted, or fresh corn kernels
1   medium zucchini or yellow squash, *diced*
3   cloves garlic, *finely minced*
1½ c. vegetarian refried black or pinto beans
5   crispy corn tostada shells

4   medium tomatoes, *chopped*
1   small red onion, *chopped*
1   bunch of cilantro, *chopped*
½   c. crumbled Mexican cheese or mild feta

Directions

1. Heat 2 tsp. oil in medium skillet. Add onion, bell peppers, corn, and zucchini/yellow squash. Cook, stirring occasionally, until vegetables are softened, about 6 minutes. Set aside.

2. Heat 1 tsp. oil in medium skillet. Add chopped garlic. Cook for 30 seconds. Add can of refried beans. Mix beans and garlic together until smooth and heated through. Set aside.

3. Spread a thin layer of the bean and garlic mixture on top of a tostada. Add a spoonful of the cooked vegetables. Top the with tomatoes, red onion, cilantro, and cheese.

4. Eat by picking up the tostada with both hands.

❋ **Tip:** *Make your own tostada shells: Spread out 5 corn tortillas on a foil lined baking sheet. Brush lightly with oil and sprinkle with salt (optional). Bake the tortillas in a preheated 400 degree oven for approximately four minutes per side, or until they are crispy and golden on each side.*

Nutrition Info *per tostada*

Total calories: 233
Carbohydrates: 37 g
Total fat: 8 g
Saturated fat: 2 g
Protein: 6 g
Fiber: 7 g
Sodium: 467 mg

Authors: Leah's Pantry

Ready In 30 min. | **Serves** 2

Sweet potatoes and black beans make a delicious, nutritious pair!

Ingredients

2	sweet potatoes or 2 russet potatoes	½	tsp. chili powder
15	oz. black beans low-sodium and rinsed	¼	tsp. salt
1	tomato diced		sour cream optional
2	tsp. olive oil		scallions chopped, optional
½	tsp. ground cumin		cilantro chopped, optional

Directions

1. Pierce potatoes in several places with a fork.

2. Bake for 40-50 minutes in a 350°F oven or microwave potatoes on high 12-15 minutes, until tender.

3. Combine beans, tomatoes, oil, cumin, chili powder, and salt. Heat in the microwave (2-3 minutes) or on the stove.

4. Slice each potato down the middle. Press open, making a well in the center.

5. Spoon the bean mixture into middle of each potato.

6. If desired, top with sour cream, scallions, or cilantro.

Nutrition Info *per 1 potato*

Total calories: 311
Carbohydrates: 57 g
Total fat: 4 g
Saturated fat: 1 g
Protein: 14 g
Fiber: 14 g
Sodium: 427 mg

Authors: Leah's Pantry

GROUND CHICKEN LETTUCE WRAPS

Ready In 20 min. **Serves** 6

Eating a Rainbow of Fruits and Vegetables is one way to get a variety of vitamins every day. In this easy recipe, ground chicken is mixed with colorful vegetables, cooked, and wrapped in crunchy green lettuce. Using lettuce to wrap cooked meats is a common practice in parts of Asia and makes for a fun and flavorful meal.

Ingredients

1   pound ground chicken
½   onion, *chopped*
Salt and black pepper, *to taste*
2   garlic cloves minced, or 1 tsp. garlic powder
1   inch piece of ginger, *peeled and minced*, or ½ tsp. ginger powder

1   c. celery, *chopped*
1   carrot, *grated*
¼   c. sesame salad dressing or teriyaki sauce
12 large outer lettuce leaves, *rinsed and patted dry*
1   tsp. red chili powder or chili flakes (optional)
¼   c. chopped peanuts (optional)

Stove Top or Skillet Directions

1. Heat 1 tbsp. oil in the bottom of a skillet.

2. Add onion and cook for 3 minutes.

3. Add garlic, ginger, celery, and ground chicken.

4. Sauté until chicken is cooked through.

5. Add carrot, dressing or sauce, and optional chili flakes. Cook for 2 more minutes.

6. Roll about ½ c. of filling into each lettuce leaf like a taco. Sprinkle with optional peanuts.

Microwave Directions

1. Microwave chicken and onion for 2 minutes.

2. Stir in garlic, ginger, and celery. Microwave 2–3 more minutes until cooked.

3. Add carrots, dressing or sauce, and optional chili flakes. Cook for 2 more minutes.

4. Roll about ½ c. filling in each lettuce leaf like a taco. Sprinkle with optional crushed peanuts.

✻   **Tip:** *You can make your own teriyaki sauce. Heat 2 tbsp. soy sauce with 1 tbsp. sugar and 1 tbsp. white vinegar in your microwave for about 1 minute. Stir to dissolve the sugar.*

Nutrition Info *per 2-wrap serving*

Total calories: 157
Carbohydrates: 6 g
Total fat: 10 g
Saturated fat: 2 g
Protein: 12 g
Fiber: 2 g
Sodium: 183 mg

Authors: Leah's Pantry

Ready In
20 min.

Serves
4

Pizza can be a nutritious, balanced meal if it's made with good ingredients. This pizza recipe uses whole wheat pita, which has more nutrients than white pizza dough. You add even more fiber and nutrients by putting plenty of fresh vegetables on top.

Ingredients

- 4 whole wheat pita bread
- 1 c. part-skim mozzarella cheese, *shredded*
- 1 c. low-sodium tomato or pizza sauce
- 1 c. vegetables, such as bell peppers, broccoli, mushrooms, olives, pineapple, onions, tomatoes, asparagus, and/or zucchini, *diced*

Directions

1. Preheat oven or toaster oven to 425°F. Line baking sheet with foil for easy cleanup.
2. Place the pitas on a baking sheet for assembly. Spread the tomato sauce on the pita leaving room for crust.
3. Sprinkle with cheese and add the toppings.
4. Cook pizzas in the oven for 5–8 minutes, or until cheese is melted.
5. Let cool for a minute before eating.

❋ **Tip:** *Use leftover veggies to cut down on prep time. Sprinkle with dried oregano, basil or chili flakes for even more flavor.*

Nutrition Info *per pita*

Total calories: 213
Carbohydrates: 32 g
Total fat: 6 g
Saturated fat: 3 g
Protein: 13 g
Fiber: 6 g
Sodium: 460 mg

Authors: Leah's Pantry

Made in the USA
Monee, IL
09 September 2024

64910594R00048